Stranger

David Punter

LEAF BY LEAF

Published by Leaf by Leaf
an imprint of Cinnamon Press
Meirion House
Tanygrisiau
Blaenau Ffestiniog
Gwynedd, LL41 3SU
www.cinnamonpress.com

ISBN: 978-1-78864-904-9

British Library Cataloguing in Publication Data. A CIP record for this book can be obtained from the British Library.

Designed and typeset in Palatino by Cinnamon Press.

Cover design by Adam Craig © Adam Craig.

Cinnamon Press is represented in the UK by Inpress Ltd and in Wales by the Books Council of Wales.

Acknowledgements

Versions of some of these poems have appeared before in *Oldhamm, Ariel, The Raven's Perch, The Kiosk, Purple Patch, Spectrum, Ink, Sweat and Tears, Labrys, PN Review, Coe Review, London Grip, Reach, Raceme, Tigershark* and *Snakeskin*. Spoken performances of some are featured on my CD, *Flashes in the Dark. Four* ('Harbour Lights', 'Echo', 'Gull' and 'Window Ghost') were anthologised in Calyx, eds Martin Rieser and Liz Cashdan (2019).

'Gull' won the inaugural Poetry Prize at the Stroud Literary Festival 2018; 'Three Kinds of Jade' was long-listed in the National Poetry Competition 2019.

The section epigraphs are translations of Sung Dynasty poems made by myself and Sun Jian of Fudan University, Shanghai.

Contents

To watch that fluttering Stranger ...

Coleridge

As St Augustine saith:
A man had rather be with his dog
than with a stranger
(whose tongue is strange unto him)

Stranger

Strange Places

An ownerless small peach tree
is blooming alone;
the vast grassland is misty and
crows are flying at daybreak;
several ruins mark out the old area
where many families used to live.

A Huai Village after the War

Sacred Country

The path cuts and blurs
    woodquake
        a litter of appearances
            torn dress stabbed with light
                hung from the shoulder

over the shoulder lies
    the dead path
        the dead follower
            hunched and lunging
                over vanishing terrain

come to the woods
    come to the graveyard
        follow newspaper
            chase Alice
                who is chasing you

behind you
    always behind you
        stab of the wood
            burning jackets
                evidence of light and death

time is shadowed loss
    a life lived twice
        abandoned
            like empty clothes
                beside a sunken road

The World's Neck

The north-west coast of Alaska,

bright and green with summer, beside a

surprisingly narrow channel, the water foaming

and speeding through the Bering Strait, tossed white;

I have brought you here to show you

the world's neck; without this flow of bright joy

the shape of oceans would change, for it is

only here that water curls upwards,

crosses the bar, rears and shouts.

                                    As we watch

a radio floats by, and then a pale blue

Volkswagen, in which there is, perhaps,

someone screaming. We are so near the edge,

but out of danger, speech drowned,

knowing the sea will freeze like a postcard

if we want it to; beside the shape

to end all shapes, on this ridiculous strand,

we are futility's jesters.

Shoreline

You could carve a poem
from the images on any single page,
like the sea slipping and sliding
amid a myriad flat rocks on the shoreline

where colours in rivulets ebb and flow
and lives are not exchanged
but lived alongside, in jags
and jets, strange inlets and escape routes

and there would be closeness of mind
and the bearings of a different language,
the eternal foreign, sliding and slipping
between the pages, along the sands

of an infinite shoreline where images,
like rocks, like water, erode and stay the same.

Harbour Lights

for Captain Smyth

I used to love seeing
the lights of the boats coming in
green and red, steering
(I could tell) a little too far
to starboard for comfort

the risk of those seamen
rounding the harbour mole
their kinship with the night
knowledge of dark things
I knew only by repute

but then I was coming in to harbour
myself and I saw the lights of land
colours too big to count
an unceasing pulse of life
and began to understand

homecoming joy, wringing
out the turtlenecks, fishermen's
friends, 'the many men
so beautiful' on coastal shelf
and resounding in the deep waters.

The Custodian in the Turner Gallery

Clouded with yellows,

       mist like a fragrance

suffused with steam.

       I try to fathom the depths.

They unfurl before me

       and close over my head,

dampening my uniform

       with distant sea-scents.

The gallery lamps

       spell out above my head

impossible messages,

       hidden in the gloom;

fighting ships

       are hull-down in the walls

and colours spread,

       like serpentine, like tar.

I am meant to observe,

       to remember;

but before these

       incandescent canvases

aflame with brine,

       soaked in fire,

I forget everything.

       I sleep, I wake.

Hecate

'I saw her again last night' (The Mamas and the Papas, 1966)

She was in Lightless Alley, amid the garbage skips
and potholes, dead violets in her hair,
fingering burnt dreams, a looseness at her hips.

Her eyes were dark as midnight, her arms so bare
I could see moonlight through them, and she spoke
a silent language that used no keening breath.

As she bent to her tasks unnumbered, the joke,
I saw, was on the living, for she knew only death
amid the syringes and phials, the stark remains

of nights of cold abandon. Just a child
of misery and ivory, dancing arabesques of drains,
amid all the glory we've defiled.

And she said her name was Hecate, goddess of the night,
mad and forever young, on a foreign shore
on the edge of limbo, on the verge of sight,
her shoulder-blades pointing to the deep earth's core.

Hadrian Rebuilds Athens

with apologies to Marguerite Yourcenar

Athens again felt the joy of activity
such as she had not known
since the age of Pericles; I was
completing what one of the Seleucids
had aspired in vain to finish,
and was making amends in kind
for the depredations of our Sulla.

To inspect the work I went daily
in and out of a labyrinth of machines
and intricate pulleys, of half-dressed columns
and marble blocks haphazardly piled,
gleaming white against the blue sky.

There was something of the excitement
of the naval shipyards; a mighty
vessel had been salvaged and was being
fitted out for the future.

Mechanics

Cholula, Mexico, 2017

Tyre shops
   and auto repairers
      flourish
on every street corner
   alongside
      taco sellers
and houses
   bright in turquoise
      pink and crimson
beyond the city
   the barrios sprawl
      sharp footsteps
making the most
   of each opportunity
      as it presents itself
hard death
   on the roads
      squeal of rubber
appeases gods
   as yet unknown
      brittle gear-cases
can always be sold
   by the mechanics
      scratching a living
by desolate streetsides
   where they dance
      the *concheros*
for a slice of bread
   informing their brothers
      about the next take
the next slide
   to oiled oblivion
      a corner too fast

a deal too slow
    a swift cut
        of knife or chiselled
cheekbone spanner
    in the works
        a skidmark
pointing to salvation
    to Maria crying
        to the children
queuing for chance
    of dice or escape
        to become what
is needed in these
    destitute times
        a mechanic.

We are Dead

We are dead.
                So let us live, and enjoy,
                                and be merry.

We died
        when the butcher killed a pig

in the market last week.

Also when that small boy
                fell into the nullah,

and hence the black candles
                in All Saints
                                at very midnight;

and in an open car
                with a senator,
                                surrounded by worshippers;

and in a small pond
                at the teeth of a minnow;

and in the ochre of battle,
                beneath the bladed wheels,

and the crazed patterns
                of holes and wire
                                against the night

sky cut with rashes,

so I say,
       let us enjoy;

for we are dead,
          and can.

Hamburg

Hamburg. Cold morning. Bright buses swaying
along the quayside. He sits at the door of the café,
all his wanderings lost in the haze. An old runner
of agents, a breed apart, always already compromised
in his own fictions of love and deceit. Far away,
there was a slow ship, a cautious voyage,
a disastrous coast; as empire crumbled, he operated
the second system, meeting her down by the fish-market,
eyes wide open and glistening;
wonderingly he observed his own fatal touch.

From the bones of the city, he spins narratives
of neglect, and promises endless riches; running
ancient rifles into Burma, eavesdropping on
burned-out spades on the Holloway Road. Everything
is information, a muscle apt for distortion;
facts and memories wind through him
and serve an unknown master.

A hunched collar, he shivers now down by the jetty,
reading the markings on the trawlers from
the heart of Africa. Waiting for something
which never happens, he flicks the gathering dust
from his cuff. Never speculate, you might drop
your guard; thinking is loss. He sees birth
only under the sign of the soft scorpion;
the rounding belly presages death.

Night gathers overhead; his ambiguous need
is to name and identify his friends.

The Twelve Haiku of Christmas

I

Pale angular light
fills out the paper-bark birch.
Is this possible?

II

Purple-laced duck, pink-
white swanstorm over the lake
bread cast in sunlight.

III

On the frosted sill
a clock of sandalwood gleams.
Time is all there is.

IV

This is what happens
night-owl smelling of cedar
hooting never stops.

V

Candles lazing on
wax drip on a paper plate
evening's tiny light.

VI

Lips parted we wait
seeing the long sharp rainbow
shade a colder life.

VII

Chimes blown in night wind
snowberry sparkle adrift,
holly, ivy. Yew.

VIII

Wanderings return
from cold abyss to firelight
burning cheeks of joy.

IX

Did you sense the truth?
Was there birth, collapse and pain
in the star-filled night?

X

The beast uncoiled limps
abjectly to the barred door.
He is admitted.

XI

Contemplate it all:
gold, and frankincense, and myrrh.
Pay for what you take.

XII

At last a mercy.
Body forgiven, and soul
untwined, released; soft.

Strange People

My clothes are covered in dust and wine stains,
I have enjoyed myself immensely wherever
I have been on the long journey.

I wonder whether I should be a poet
entering the Sword Gate
on a donkey when it is drizzling.

Journeying to the Sword Gate Pass in Drizzle

Road Runner

I saw the road runner at my door,

and he said, 'This road has murdered me

by stealth and outside the sun's glint;

avenge me'. And I thought on his words

(when he had faded); they washed around

outside me, filling the slanted spaces

of trust and landscape. I felt them slide

against me, and mould to a preconception;

and felt them ebb, myself struggling,

hands upreached, arms plunging into

the seeming spaces, trying to grasp.

Then they were gone; and I was running,

the road foaming on my chest

as the words glittered on the highest pine,

and I, repressible, caught below,

reached an ever-closed door, and said:

Jimmy the Pig

Jimmy the pig
hits town metal
belt bare tattooed
arms brawling for
a fight denim low
slung jeans boots
crushing the sidewalk

Jimmy the pig
looking for coons pakis
brow tense jaw
unsmiling eighteen winters
union jack teeshirt
bastards go home
kicking the brown slush

Jimmy the pig
festooned with light
caught in the early
morning glare arrows
through and through that
meagre ornate body
racked with resolution

Jimmy the pig.

Pushover

Face off. A young man, teeshirt,

short sleeves, trim muscles bulging,

scalp like a bullet. His girl-friend

behind the push-chair, fag sticking

straight out from pale stretched lips.

He pushes an older man, a drunk

who's been shouting abuse

(or some such, I'm not that close),

who staggers and falls, a ragged

scarf unfurling from his throat

like a flag of generational defeat

and the bruiser struts away, the girl

trailing defiantly behind, fag still

immobile, the baby a silent witness.

The Whisperer

Sir, wash your hands;
outside they are demanding a body, a head,
a corpse, well-hung—
would you like me to procure one, sir?
My third cousin
is out around the city late at night,
he knows the quick slice, the violet knife.
This could all be so much easier
if you would let me
help you, sir.

Spoleto, 1500

My lady, they will
worry if they taste the dregs; far better
to let me wash them down
with good wine,
fine sauces, *tartare, meunière*—
will you not sample, good lady?
These golden dishes are, I assure you,
for your delight alone—would I deceive you, dear lady,
I who know the consequences all too well?

Tenochtitlán, 1519

O divine one,
lord of the planets
and conquistador of the New Jerusalem,
let not these savages assail
the clarity of your conscience
under God; you did what you had to do
and anyway, their weapons are mislaid
or rusted from the elbow to the hip.
These unclean men
will suffer from history's whip.

House of Commons, 2019

And you, honourable ladies
and gentlemen, ventriloquising
sordid messages of hate
across an empty chamber,
do not worry about the dying,
the addicted, the infirm;
I can find means of putting all this to rest.
Let then scrabble for a pittance,
lie back, enjoy
your immunity from fear or pain.

Echo

I know that I asked you to join with me
I remember it well—we were much younger then
I never thought to give you the key.
> *The key. The key. The key.*

I thought you were an Abyssinian maid
whose music would lull me to sleep and beyond
but now I just want to go out and get laid.
> *Echo. Echo. Echo.*

I loved the way your hair melted like gold
and the shift of your eyes from turquoise to grey
but now they're faded and the truth must be told.
> *Be told. Be told. Be told.*

I believed it all, whatever I said,
but you thought it was you I was speaking to
when really the voice was inside my own head.
> *Echo. Echo. Echo.*

And I still see me as I stare in the pool,
a perfection of image that none can destroy
an unravaged surface, the essence of cool.
> *Of cool. Of cool. Of cool.*

But don't weep. my darling, there's no need to cry
there's water enough in the pool as it is
I have myself; you have earth, wind and sky.
> *Echo. Echo. Echo.*

A Quiet Life

It was when, in the brightening mornings,

awake as a sentinel, he could hear no birdsong

and when, in the narrowing evenings,

newscasters' voices rang across hollow distances.

The audiologist was grave in pinstripes and goatee,

spoke of 'inner damage'; the hearing aids

offered only tinny radio sounds

that didn't overcome the roar inside his ears.

Now people think him stupid; and he lives

a life of dignified pain. A quiet life.

Clear Light 1

Dimly
    I can manipulate the shadows
    I create half-worlds
        from full images

You beneath my pillow
    (kept but not entered)
        breathed into me
           clear light
              to wash my images
                fresh

I could perhaps have
    loved
        you—I am not
           strong yet—
              but you were filled
                with remembrance of my
                    clear light

I feel shot through
    with blue and purple
        my creations
           rearing
              in soft devotion

Once I was a woman
    and will be
        again
           when the salt of my creation
              dissolves in your
                still persistent
                clear light

When Last I was Lost

When last I was lost in your eyes

and in the impure silences behind those dreams

I had of you in my fingertip mind;

I walked, missing from my thoughts,

through a receding chapel, treading

your straw not yet deserted

and saw handprints of the yet to come

on the altar; three genuflecting saints,

one looking pinioned within, one without,

the third at the likelihood of my arrival.

He had trees in his arms, and a

bashful smile, and a flaked stone cross

horizontal between his legs.

You are not protected by yourself

but by the forms

of those to come,

candles behind a screen.

Wish upon a Star

with respect to Emily Dickinson

I wish I was a teddy bear
    I wish I was a dove
I wish my girl-friend was alive
    I wish I was in love

I wish I hadn't done to her
    what she wished to do to me—
or so my fancy told me—
    and then I would not be

locked in this dreadful singular—
    there could be two not one—
but blood will have its own
    and what is done is done

For Miss Caulker

I find your sparseness

intensely moving; bleached rib, blowing

down the strand, last leaf, beginning to

make sense; blocked. In March,

your month, there was a tea-party

of stones, and we sucked the telegraph wires

dry. You are time-honoured; in the future

there is palsy, and also a thin crystal, from which,

slowly, you will be unpacked; as your sap

streams down to the sea.

In the Garden of Yu

Shanghai, 1983, 2019

A thousand goldfish radiate in the pool before

the Hall of the Jade Mountain; then spin towards the bread you've thrown

packing themselves in deep below the rose stone. On the bridge

of Nine Corners thin shadows hover, carved in bone,

smoke grey and cloud pink. Stepping through the Dragon Door,

you feel the garden remaking itself around you, each delicate edge

adjusted in the Hall of Perfect Harmony; I can place you

in a myriad settings, moving from one intricate lattice

to another. In the Hall of the Three Ears of Grain

there are antlers, and each chair is a crimson sculpted chalice

to hold you, poised. Tiny floating trees, misted with blue,

are your attendants, ripples in the pathways and the scrolled wood's stain

deferentially record your every movement. When you stop,

the garden waits a little; then the Hall of Crafted Singing

opens like an offering hand, and the tenuous trees quiver.

Like rain, and your reflection caught in every drop,

the antique music comes, and with it the deer springing

from the mountains to you, across Yu's clear and bounding river.

Strange Creatures

Why must I feel the depths of nostalgia
in the last days of spring,
to dress my hair in time of sickness is
of all things the most annoying.

The swallows on the beam are twittering all day long,
soft winds send the fragrance of roses through the blinds.

The Last Days of Spring

Gull

We've got 'em bang to rights, the noisy screamers
and harbingers of our oceanic discontent;
Jonathan Livingston, George Barker, Chekhov,
fish and chips, snatched sandwiches, a certain
stink of half-remembered, half-digested fish.

Forgetting how huge they are is one thing; worse
is forgetting how *gull* they are, how unlike
anything else in the many wild kingdoms we
pompously incline to regard as our home despite
the anarchy of mosquito, buzzard, lynx.

A white head endangered among rocks, scrabbling
claws spread to meet the gust, there is nothing
romantic about this unseasoned life, bare feed
and guano, profitless, enduring, cold
as midnight, we think, is cold; but always cold.

In moments we are gull, instances of dream,
flapping from the black precipice, swooning
in the down-draught, knowing no knowledge
except the squawking mouths, the endless need
revealed for a second in cowl of black and grey.

        endangered among rocks

                instances of dream

   squawking mouths

                  wild kingdoms

        enduring, cold

            the black precipice

    oceanic discontent

          half-remembered, half-digested

   cowl of black and grey

Cormorant

The harbour is studded with small floats—

plastic containers, anything that will

hold an orange rope. I walk past

as a small boy points over my shoulder

asking his father, 'What's that?'

'An albatross'. An albatross?

I swing round in amazement and see

nothing to begin with. Then,

perched on a floating pink beach ball,

spectral black, wings outstretched,

elegantly keeping balance,

not an albatross. A cormorant.

Have I been the victim of a joke,

or seen a vision? How to choose ...

Albatross

The Eagle and the Jaguar

It doesn't matter how many times

the guide tells you, 'These are images

of peace and harmony', you still stand

on the parched plain of Chichen Itza

staring at the grey outline of tooth and claw

and are drawn back to a violent world,

the decapitated players on the ball-game frieze,

the stained bowls, the obsidian knives

in the museum where Maya and Toltec

effigies recede through screens of history

blood-boltered, fastened to the ground

with stone, the feathered serpents gaping

open-mouthed at the pyramid's foot,

memories of flame haunting the scrubland.

Crabs

The crabs come
over the harbour wall.
They are small

and green and they strut
and scuttle
like tiny engines.

They mean no malice,
and are not of our world;
but it is too late.

Tiny pincers are growing
from the corners
of our eyes, and these

will only increase
in size until we become
violent and blind.

The Dull Anvil

Black

yolk

runs

within

the

yellow

egg.

Woodpecker-sound

betrays

the

dried-out

shell.

A Cold Morning

Icicles surround

the bone-cold stallion

of morning.

Angled fence-posts

not yet begun

their creaking dance.

Chalk men

approach

on frosty mud.

Fields, coverlets

rippling with

unconnected pattern.

A generator

howls through its teeth

in a lonely shed.

When not Absorbed

When not absorbed in solving
    complex mathematical problems
rabbits mostly eat grass.

Between measuring the air
    with scythes of feathered fingers
swifts swim in the downdraught.

Describing impossible geometries
    in twenty-seven dying languages
evening weasels hunt upon the road.

Gone in the eye of the blink
    (headlamp, motion, gorse)
owls devote themselves to the Bible.

Crow-lenses are efficacious
    over leagues of heaving earth
where the stars stop for a rest.

When stationary before their gods
    and engaged on Einstein's mechanics
foxes spare a thought for their prey.

Mr Punch

A clotted history of mountebanks and fit-ups,
the shining Crocodile consumes the bloated sausage,
Lithuanian 'professors' adapt their tale
to narratives of forgotten invasions.

'Where's the babby, Mr Punch? Where's the babby?'
Oh, don't you worry your pretty little head about that—
he's safe, very safe—on griddle or at the sharpened end
of a rolling pin. I have my little ways.

Sometimes ridicule is all that works, sometimes
we need the caricature of ages, as the constellations
are, weirdly, cartoons of the endless variety
of the night sky. The Crocodile laughs again.

Is this the Skeleton dancing? Is this Death coming,
or is it the Devil? He'll be no match for me.
Lumpen, brazen, full of mother courage,
I go on insulting, assaulting. You, my man, are me.

Ghost

Phantasmal, ragged, laughing,
I stride out along the street behind you.
Unshaped, prescient, whippet-formed,
I cavort in the road before you.

You are so solid, I giggle:
clothed, buried in tumultuous flesh.
Yet you shall be as I am—
free, dissolute, distraught.

Do not imagine rest;
I am mine own perturbary
and you, before night's end
will be bereft of every protestation.

I could float off on the dry wind
but I prefer it here; my game,
my *politesse* demands it;
I live to serve you, my master.

I curlicue, I swindle, I cheat,
you know full well I will—
there is no upright bone in my
boneless body. Praise the Lord.

Belonging to the sinister persuasion
I have no time for the living;
leave that to the dull corporeal
and come. Caper with me.

Window Ghost

We are gathered
a crowd of unknowing
some all night, they say,
some since bird-yellow dawn
tautened strings

a broad shop window
empty, paused, waiting
There, cries the boy,
There: a shade of violet,
bending, shimmering

we strain and peer—
was there a movement
ripple in the glass
fault, parallax, water
between the sheets

an impossible change in the air
a defunct TV screen
emitting its final rays
blue as paradise,
faint as the last bird

we saw nothing, we say
even to the police, moving us
along, an unseemly crowd
nothing, except perhaps
the ghost's violet shimmer.

Strange Objects

It is like a ridge when viewed horizontally,
and like a peak vertically;
it is not the same seen nearby or from a distance,
from above or below.

I cannot see the true
colours of Mount Lu simply
because I am staying on it.

Inscribed on the Wall of the Xi Lin Temple

A Feather Boa

Dance with the blind,

    shall we,

        at the end of the world?

Come, a landing-stage,

    a withered tree,

        the dark lake;

what else

    do we need?

      The stage is set,

        and the oak has shed

her branches.

      What was penned in the oak?

          Why,

Sycorax—

    but she has escaped,

        in time

for Christmas.

      Dark November,

        falling of leaves,

a pleasure-boat on the rippled surface.

         Let us think,

          my love.

      Frozen with memory.

Iridium Flare

Iridium was named for the goddess Iris, deity of rainbows.
It occurs rarely on earth, although the sudden flaring
of iridium has been observed throughout the solar system.

Rainbows are all circular;
circumpolar stars move visibly to the naked eye;
circles within circles, slipping discs,
an intricate instrumentation
available to astrolabe and the violet screen.

The sky divides into parallelograms
and classes, imaginary deities
lounge on milky beds, the stars
are silk and satin, spongy memory
of other days, deep time.

And through it all goes
an eye-splitting dagger of light,
silver-purple, momentary, sharp
in its dismantling of the heavens'
gentle, incomprehensible symmetry.

Boat

I call to mind this boat
blue-painted she is
marooned on greying sands
far from the purple sea

Her name is

> scratched are her bows
> her gunwales blistered
> and pocked like time
> and her small trim deckhouse

has ceased to vibrate

There will be creatures
at home in her fallen rigging
they gesticulate of loss
and the ending of her sea-haul

Her name is

> she has ceased to level
> and she is awash
> with dry memories
> of thwarted journeyings

Dried rust falls
to the sands beneath
and her masts are toppled
with a redolence of climbers

Her name is

Mixing with Vodka

Almond

juice of apricot stone

fluid white

encompassing a small

transparency

keenly bounded, like egg-white:

then dissolving rush.

I see your hand

tremble.

Paperbark Birch

For seventeen years now, your fragility
has enmeshed me; your perpendicular
tracery shapes my dreams, gives oriels
to my imaginings. Every morning
your shed branches give bright fresh colour
to hedge and lawn; fragments of parchment bark
suggest an impenetrable pristine writing.

I wonder ceaselessly what messages
are inscribed on the underside of white,
what charted forms, and shapes of land and coast
stare up at my unreading, unwise eye.
These arrows, should I follow in their course,
these creases, do they form a book of life
to give shape to the the shapeless, darkness lighting?

Cascades of papyrus, nature's Möbius strips
litter the green; I crawl among the lanes
and avenues of code without a book.
Writing for the blind; a grand summation
of all experience blown by the wind,
flesh stripped from bone, dry husks without the juice,
paper and bark are one in the blue dawn's sighting.

Newport Sands: The Jellyfish

Stranded on the stones in shades of grey

and pink. 'D'you think that it's alive or dead?',

said Jez, and so before the end of day

we were all wondering whether hope had fled

or was rescued by the sight of this sad stray,

with us revitalised to carry on our way,

since 'We must rescue it!', exclaimed young Ned

full of conviction, something in his head

persuading him that this was all we had

standing between us and a slow collapse

like tentacles unfurling, or like the sad

seepage of colours through unsightly gaps

in all our lives—we could not now be glad;

the creature's death would alter all our maps.

The Ordinary Perfect Journey

And so, this is a train.

    The *koan* of wheels slides off endlessly,

        reminiscence of torture in the twilight

the slow chains thudding

    and a luminous divided body waiting to be born.

It is gold and azure in the courtyard.

    The thronged hum of emptiness

        glimmering all around. We do not know

with what consummate serenity

    we shall in the end emerge

        into her arms, crucified in the arches' glitter.

And then there is this blue blush of grapeseed

    staring from the fallen flesh,

    the face of bemusement

sliding unaccommodated among the silent hoardings

    as, again, this is a train.

Three Kinds of Jade

Jadeite

In Guatemala, light green 'quetzal',
treasured by the Olmec and the Maya,
also apple-green, greenish white,
occasionally blue or violet.
Also the Burmese variant so highly
valued by the Chinese emperors,
forged into weapons, never for use,
always for ceremonial exchange.

Nephrite

So-called because 'green gold'
was once reckoned a cure for kidney stones,
also 'tomb jade' and 'grave jade',
hard as steel. River jade flows
from the Kuen-Lun Mountains
through the markets of Khatan,
more prized than silver, and in NZ is
passed off as Maori to gullible tourists.

Dying Horse

The parson's horse, Sterne tells us,
was 'as lean, and as lank, and as sorry
a jade' as could be found, and Austen
shows us a 'cursed broken-winded jade',
but it is the bad-tempered women
who abound in Shakespeare and Fielding;
though perhaps they are merely tired,
wearied, fatigued; not prized like gold.

The Mohs Scale:

The Progress of a Relationship

A scale of mineral hardness;
Friedrich Mohs (1812) partly following Theophrastus and Pliny the Elder

1: Talc

Beginning with baby powder, softness leaks
into the mineral hard, assuring all
that however the carapace forms, there will still be
enough reminder to occasion fall.

2: Gypsum

But as we get to know each other better
we need a certain definition felt;
as fertiliser, or as blackboard chalk,
we cannot let the growing mineral melt.

3: Calcite

Egyptian alabaster, onyx-marble,
our bodies grow in texture before our eyes.
They harden now, as we break apart their mantle—
that moving form that hurts us with its cries.

4: Fluorite

And now we start on colour and enamel,
our joinings open to ultraviolet light;
optics to see into the far distance
where the hard also becomes the very bright.

5: Apatite

This name means 'deceiving' or 'misleading';
often mistaken, nothing to call its own.
Yet all we see is a coloured crystal bleeding
a light too dagger-perfect yet to hone

6: Orthoclase feldspar

And here is where the igneous rocks begin,
and also uranium, where all fission starts—
strength and fracture parented as one,
they join and break our fates and loins and hearts.

7: Quartz

Steel and emerald, finest of stones, reflect
our industry and ornament arrayed
as in a marriage's cornucopiac display
of jewels, girders, beauty, wealth and trade.

8: Topaz

But all topaz that we value is corrupted,
for topaz has no colour of itself;
green, blue and pink, they all are added measures
to help us, as now we harden on the shelf.

9: Corundum

Ruby for red, for shed drops at the crossroads;
sapphire for blue, as blue as blue can be.
And sandpaper to abrade and smooth the hardness,
to rasp against the gems, to make them free.

10: Diamond

The harshness and the value hand in hand,
alone now with the drill bit, the burglar's tool,
the bloodshed and the vault, the king of kings;
come, let us salute the empty, shining jewel!

Strange Conditions

I am leaning on the rail alone while
wind and rain blow over the lake,
the mountain looks like the twelve coiled buns
of Lady Xiang's hair.

If only I could be on the surface of the lake
viewing the green mountains through the
mountainous silver breakers.

Mounting Yue Yang Tower in the Rain to Look at Mount Jun

How can the Hedgerows

How can the hedgerows
    and the purple of the bluebells
memories like rabbits
    scuttling off the path
or like swallows
    criss-crossing ahead of the car
on tracks, always on tracks
    a flash of fur
as a weasel pounces
    a sliver of dark light
in rain-diamonded undergrowth
    a brilliant unforgetting
of old ways, never hidden
    but memoried as a small boy
in school uniform
    lost by a dark lake
on the edge of the swamp
    eyes wide for what
might appear, nodding
    at the top of the forest
where his run might end
    before it has begun
unnoticed, unrevealed
    by the innocent hedgerows.

Back Spring

Mud cracks like snow that fell yesterday,
leaving the desecrated barracks half-built.
Up from the bone-riddled ground they come,
lozenges, red-tawny tombstones,

changing colours as they rise, verdant with
age, springy with youth, each one a new
challenge to death, not to be smoothed away,
they resist the downward heave of the spade.

But they can furl, leap back, unburied memories,
onto the trees like caterpillars; they have no
bounds, they scatter seeds like rain, we jump
as soldiers to their sad command.

The Lights of Glass

for Thomas Traherne, Tom Denny and Douglas Traherne Harding

in Hereford Cathedral

God had before made an Epistle of his love

So love is born in writing, in the golden love letter

where each flourish gestures towards an uplift,

the soul awaiting its consummation beyond

this postponement, this delay, which is the breach

between lovers, their continuing non-present,

the not-being-there, the magic conjuring that

eliminates absence, prolongs innocence, allows

bluetits and starlings to sing of the ineffable.

He had written it upon the earth in knots and flowers

And perhaps there is a beckoning, a summoning

to worlds beyond ours, places and nests where all

colours are one and yet marvellously differentiated

in hues and tints obedient yet resistant

to the artist's rainbow; we would so love to estimate

the range between violet and purple, but such is not

given to us, even among the manifold gifts we have

which excite a gratitude beyond all fixity of time.

In bloody characters in the living creatures

Nothing remains the same; all eats or is eaten. Bombasts
of plumage cover a wild disdain for the brutish facts—
reproduce or die; nothing must or can stand in the way
as we stare across the motorway at another meaty smash
and would wait until the ambulances die away
except that we have another place to be—office, dinner,
assignation, some known, some secret, all written on our
flesh, letters to pass through some unimaginable censor.

Which was in more bloody characters afterwards copied

Everything is real; nothing is permitted. Our tyrants are simulacra,
they ape the power they once had in shirts of steel, blind
passageways where doom kicks up a fuss, and people's courage mocks
the petty fantasies of totality. Nature is copy, root and branch,
without it we would be footloose, unanchored, lost in space
without the peril of a singular agony, by means of which alone
we can assure ourselves that the letter will survive, that
the ancient intimate call of one to one will finally pass the test.

In the death of his Son

It has nothing to do with religion; the true and dreadful impiety
is that the child might predecease the parents, calling out, naked
and in pain on some dusty road, or in some gaudy whorehouse,
saying, yes, 'Why hast thou forsaken me?', yet we were never given
a promise. No voice from on high, no postponed, undelivered
letter contained an exemption clause, we were never told
it would be fair. Yet it is right to have hopes—the thrushes and the
magpies say this to us in their screams and foragings.

At Dusk

Whitened grass and deeply pinkened clover

shapes collapse and show their own reserve.

The ancient tumulus lurches and turns over

settling life's journey in a different groove.

Silhouettes of love, shadows of flavour,

no black and white, just widely haloed grey.

The girl at dusk wears a mallow for a favour

glinting vermilion in the sun's last ray.

No drum is beaten, no violin's last glory,

no maddened clarinet assaults the sense;

the pause prolongs the finish of the story:

A pitch-black army pitches night's black tents.

1st April 2019

In the i newspaper, deputy editor Andrew Webster invites us to pick out the April Fool headline. I found (perhaps unluckily) thirteen contenders.

Licence to krill: US plans to turn fish into spies

Facebook has too much power, admits Zuckerberg

Saudis 'hacked phone of Amazon chief'

Berlusconi to stand in European election

'Biggest ever' rise in living wage

PM to seek fourth vote on Brexit deal

Hard to swallow: British biscuits axed by Brexit

PM could ask the Queen to block MPs' Brexit plan

Teachers to be held accountable on knife crime

Fairy shots [photographs] under the hammer

Comedian leads poll in vote for next president

Cows 'valued over women'

Free turmeric for the over 50s

Half-Lies

We are not breaking away

>we are forging a new future

We are not risking our children

>we are full of bold adventure

We are not destroying jobs

>we are creating opportunities

We are not against foreigners

>we respect their contribution

We are not post-imperial

>we are a New Order

We are not rife with prejudice

>we see the colours of truth

We are not arms dealers

>we are purveyors of freedom

We are not full of shit

>we just enjoy telling lies

Clear Light 2

Clear light
made   you
city girl
city   recusant   now
made   laugh
in a clear stream
for laughing.

I would have
your   laugh
on a golden salver
but it   would spill
become venomous   with keeping.

Made   cry
for the life-killer
by form   and not   by purpose
city   habits
lying by a pool
green.

Clear light
made   you   when
apples and pears and cherries and a sparrow
in my eyes
winked
through   the portal   of never.

And I   would steal
clear light
if it were not
doubly   sanctified
to you   and in the   remembrance
of you
made light.

Vulcan

At his old tricks again, spitting lava
down the steep of the innocent mountain,
rearing skyward, the sun disappearing
behind the bars and lattices of the night.

Or roaring 'Fire Down Below'
as the mainmast's rigging crashes in flame
and the magazine splits its sides
in the torrential laughter of the burning.

Or the flamethrower slashing
a body in two as the walls cave in
and scorched blocks collapse
in the city where nothing stands.

First he kept the wolves at bay,
warmed cooking-pots, gave the family
a hearth of affection, guarded against
the storm's bitterness and woe.

Then we found him better uses,
turned him to tasks of division—
What is born of the flame shall perish
of the flame, and not be healed.

Janus the two-faced is pallid

beside these flickering images

firelit, dying by candlelight, of Vulcan,

always rearing at the back of the cave.

Three of Wands

loosely extrapolated from the Tarot

Established strength. Trade, commerce,
discovery. Ships crossing the sea.
Reversed, the end of troubles.

And by extension:

Departure and homecoming. Transits
of unaccustomed planets. A wakeful
defender in marsh or fen.

And then again:

Empire and its downfall. Liberation
of a suffering earthbound peasantry.
Revolution and circles of fire.

Again we throw the cards:

History rewritten. The untroubledness
of majestic polluted seas.
Dark joy in ravishment.
Agony of the oppressor, writhing
on the thorn of the oppressed.

New Alphabet

for André Breton

algorithm

    the beautiful dockmaster

cosmophobia

    de-tailed disarticulation

ecstatic rocking heart

    a fantastic outering

Gongoratta the Thin

    his face a welter of cheek-bones

ideality of the dextrosinister

    Jade Emperor with no head

kenosis

    longing, longing

martyrs to the overwhelming dead

    netscapes of clothed fish

ophidectomies, snakeskin boots

    pond hospital

quadrupeds *in absentia*

    the ridicule of nations

sulphur-blue and pearl-purple

    the Triple Fountain

under the grey hill, through the black rock

    a vexed and shadowy carapace

words disturbed like crustaceans of sand in a rock-pool

    xenophagic impulse

Yolande, submit

    zilch for your comfort